Intentional Youth Ministry

Matt Moore

Copyright © 2019 Matthew Moore

All rights reserved. Written permission must be secured from the publisher to use or reproduce any part of this book, except for brief quotations.

Scripture quotations marked NIV are from THE HOLY BIBLE, NEW INTERNATIONAL VERSION®, NIV® Copyright © 1973, 1978, 1984, 2011 by Biblica, Inc.® Used by permission. All rights reserved worldwide.

The Message is quoted: scripture taken from The Message. Copyright © 1993, 1994, 1995, 1996, 2000, 2001, 2002. Used by permission of NavPress Publishing Group.

Scripture quotations marked (NLT) are taken from the Holy Bible, New Living Translation, copyright © 1996, 2004, 2007 by Tyndale House Foundation. Used by permission of Tyndale House Publishers, Inc., Carol Stream, Illinois 60188. All rights reserved.

ISBN: 9781096874522

DEDICATION

This book is dedicated to the mentors who have helped me become the man and leader I am today. Brad Ruff, Adam McCain, and Randy Bezet. Thanks for seeing potential in me and calling it out.

Intentionality has the power to change everything. In *Intentional Youth Ministry*, Matt Moore offers youth pastors and leaders a fresh approach to effectively impacting the next generation by simply being intentional. Through thought provoking questions and real-life experiences, youth pastors and leaders will find practical insight that explains the value of intentionality and encourages them to lead intentionally.

-Randy Bezet
Lead Pastor Bayside Community Church
Bradenton, FL

"Intentional youth ministry isn't just another inspirational book. It really is a practical guide that will help you move beyond impression to impact. If you're looking to build something bigger than yourself, this is a great resource to help you do just that."

-Anthony O'Neal
NY Times Best Selling Author & Ramsey Personality
Nashville, TN

"Matt Moore is one of the most trusted voices in America when it comes to student ministry. I love his insight and innovation and a phenomenal student ministry has been the fruit. You will no doubt be blessed by not only his words, but his passion and heart."

-Dan Lian
Teaching Pastor, Newspring Church
Anderson, SC

"After 17 years in youth ministry I've explored just about every model of youth ministry under the sun with one main goal in mind, I wanted to help students reach their full potential in Jesus. Unfortunately, many of those models were missing a key ingredient, which was intentionality of what a student would "become" as a result of those ministry efforts. Many of the models helped get students to an event or a service but I still felt like we were missing the mark or maybe even failing to accomplish the mission.

To be candid, I wish I could rewind time and take the wisdom from Matt's book and apply it because I'm sure it would save me many frustrations from failed attempts to reach students for Jesus.

I've heard it once said that "many ministries end up somewhere but few ministries end up somewhere on purpose." If you want your ministry and the students you are leading to end up somewhere on purpose, then I highly recommend this book as a resource. Matt is one of the most effective Student Pastors I've ever witnessed that has served this generation well and for the long haul."

- JASON LAIRD
Lead Pastor, Sozo Church
San Francisco, CA

Matt Moore

CONTENTS

	Introduction	3
1	Intentional Chaos	7
2	Intentional Separation	14
3	Intentional Philosophy	27
4	Intentional Experiences	38
5	Intentional Growth	70
6	Intentional Leadership	82
7	Intentional Discipleship	90
8	Intentional Evaluation	97
9	Intentional Structure	107
10	Intentional Longevity	116

ACKNOWLEDGMENTS

Thanks to my amazing wife Angie who has believed in me and supported me in this endeavor. I love you!

To my kids Aiden and Audrey who teach me every day how to be more intentional. I love you both.

Thanks to Randy and Amy Bezet and the leadership of Bayside Community Church. For believing in your team and allowing them to live out their full God given purpose.

Thanks to Nate Fox for graphic and cover work.

Introduction

Consider this scenario which sadly is happening in youth ministries throughout the nation. An unchurched student walks into the youth service for the first time, and no one even says hello. The band is still onstage practicing, and shortly thereafter it proceeds into the worship set, which is not only sloppy but full of churchy lingo that makes no sense to most of your churched students, let alone someone who has never been to church. The student stands there because everyone else is. They feel uncomfortable and out of place, waiting and hoping that it's going to get better soon. But it only gets more uncomfortable as worship comes to an end and someone jumps onstage to welcome students, play a game, and pump the crowd. The problem is that the person trying to hype up the students is so uncomfortable onstage that now they have everyone in the audience feeling uncomfortable. They proceed with a game that isn't explained well and ends up being a disaster. So they continue by welcoming all first-time guests and having them stand, only to make the new student feel even more uncomfortable. Then it's time for the message, so the youth pastor jumps onstage and begins to preach a 30-40 message, but somewhere between "What's up, everyone?" and the closing prayer they've lost most of the students in the room. Not necessarily because they didn't have something valid to say, but because of the way they said it. So they say their prayer and the service comes to an end. This student who decided to give the service a try is now eagerly waiting for their parents to come pick them up so they can get the heck out of there. Not only was excellence lacking, but no one even made an effort to connect with them while they were there. Maybe, just maybe, as a result of this student's experience, they never walk into the doors of another church.

Sound a little over the top? I don't believe that it is! Too often there is little to no intentionality in our student ministries. They aren't accomplishing their purpose, and quite possibly that's because we don't even know the purpose ourselves.

Student ministry can be one of the most effective and life-changing ministries within the church. Unfortunately, it's easy to fall into the routine of doing youth ministry the way it's always been done, never stopping to ask the question, "Why are we doing what we are doing?" I think that if we take a good hard look at the majority of youth ministries in the majority of churches around the country, and the world for that matter, we'll find that more often than not, student ministries are being done with little to no intentionality. There is the fly-by-the-seat-of-your-pants or shotgun approach to youth ministry. We throw someone in with our students and call them a youth pastor even though they have no clue what they are doing and, even worse, no calling. So in reality it becomes babysitting or entertainment, which is a huge injustice to the young people in our church. Or maybe we are called to do youth ministry, but we aren't equipped to do it with excellence. When I first was getting my feet wet in youth ministry I had a passion for young people, but to be honest I had very little knowledge of how to effectively reach and pastor them. There really wasn't a whole lot of intentionality in what I was doing. I was just trying to figure things out as I went. Looking back, I wish that I had understood the concept of doing youth ministry with intentionality.

My hope and prayer is that this book will help you to start looking at your student ministries with more intentionality. So that you can effectively reach the students God has called you to reach.

1

Intentional Chaos

If you've been a part of youth ministry for any period of time, you understand that it can be a little bit chaotic. If you're just starting out in youth ministry, this will soon be your reality: the emotional roller coaster ride that is the teenage life, the inconsistency that most students experience at home, the identity crises, dating, and, well…the drama!

Young people have enough chaos in their lives without being part of a student ministry that adds to it.

I have walked into multiple youth services and attended youth events that could only be described as chaotic. The worship team is still onstage rehearsing, even as students begin to arrive (if they practice at all). The worship experience is so all over the place and sloppy that it actually distracts from worship. Students aren't engaged in worship; in fact, they are talking or texting during that time because it's actually painful to listen to, let alone participate in. Too often in the church world we make comments like, "Worship is about Him, and as long as the Holy Spirit moves in the service, that's all that matters." Listen…by all means we want to give God freedom to move in the hearts of students, but that has too often become an excuse for us to do things without excellence. Some person jumps onstage to welcome the students who is a horrible communicator, and while they may have a great heart and be great with students, that doesn't mean they should have a microphone in their hand. We play some game that hasn't really been explained to the person leading it, so they in turn don't explain it to the students participating, and it's a big flop. We get up and preach a message that is too long, too boring, irrelevant, and the entire time we are speaking over students who are chatting. We say a little prayer for salvation at the end of service, but don't have any next steps for students who want to grow in their walk with God. Our leadership team consists of anyone who is willing to help out, even if they have no heart or passion for students. We speak on topics that have no relevance to issues students are facing in this season of their lives. We had a youth event planned, with details posted on our church website, listed in the bulletin, and promoted on social media, but we decided to cancel at the last minute and didn't communicate it to everyone, so now we have to deal with the aftermath.

I remember my second year in youth ministry, when I led my first group of students on a missions trip to Mexico. A handful of high school students were on that trip, and, never having led a group of students on a missions trip like this before, I neglected to think about all the details ahead of time. So we flew into south Texas, where we were going to be picked up and driven across the border. Problems began before we ever left the States, though. I'd made the assumption that our high school students could be responsible for their own passports. So we got through security at the airport and stopped to use the restroom. About five minutes later, as we were headed to meet our party, I heard a student in the back say, "I can't find my passport." Those words haunt me to this day! We spent the next hour or so combing the airport without any luck. So here I was, looking like a fool because I was meeting with other groups and pastors and now I was the rookie who let a student lose their passport. The reality wasn't that this high school student was irresponsible; I was just unorganized. Students have enough chaos in their lives without us adding to it.

Man in the Mirror

I don't want to spend too much time now on intentionality in our service and event environments. For now I want to turn the focus on the youth pastor or leader. As John Maxwell says, "Everything rises and falls on leadership." I believe the first place we have to look if we are experiencing chaos in our ministry area is at the person leading it. Many have misconceptions about identifying and evaluating a youth pastor. Since when is the main qualification for pastoring young people being a goofball?

I mean, seriously…I remember my early years of doing youth ministry, feeling pressure to try to be this goofy, crazy, bounce-off-the-walls kind of guy. I actually believed that the success of the ministry somehow was related to how crazy I was. By all means you want someone relevant, but what makes somebody relevant isn't necessarily personality alone. Students want authenticity. They want relationships. They don't want someone to pretend to be somebody or something they're not. A mentor of mine once told me, "Don't be a superstar and not a father." Those words stuck with me and have affected the way I do student ministry.

For too long youth pastors have had this stigma. Something gets broken at the church during a youth service, and people say, "He's just a youth pastor." Some student gets left behind at the church after a youth service, and we say, "Oh, well, that's just what youth pastors do." A youth event is completely disorganized and chaotic, and we let it go, saying, "Well you know youth pastors just aren't that organized." It's bad enough that those generalizations have been made about youth pastors, but too often we live up to them. We just accept that it's OK to be disorganized and all over the place. Why is it that we get a pass or give ourselves one? Being a youth pastor is one of the greatest callings there is. We have the opportunity to help mold the lives of young people. One day we will stand before God and give an account of how faithful we were with our calling and how well we pastored the students God entrusted us with. I would hate to look Jesus in the eye and give the excuse, "I was just a youth pastor."

Organization isn't the enemy of student ministry! In fact, it might very well be the missing link in your ministry area. "God is no respecter of persons," and I don't believe I have experienced success in student ministry because I am more called than others, or because God loves or favors me any more than He does anyone else. I do, however, believe that God has blessed the organization and intentionality with which I have done student ministry. Chaos is part of student ministry. Let's just make sure it's organized chaos!

I promise you, your leadership will appreciate it, your volunteers will thrive, the parents of your students will LOVE you, and your student ministry will be more effective and intentional.

2
Intentional Separation

Time to tackle the age-old question: "Should I do middle school and high school ministry together or separately?"

Combining student ministries has become commonplace in most churches across the country. A lot of churches do middle school and high school together, and some have even added college into the mix. And this is not just limited to small churches. In the past it seemed that the larger your church grew, the more likely it was to separate its youth ministries. That's not the case anymore;

a growing number of larger churches have been combining student ministries. To be honest with you, this is something I have felt strongly about since I first started out in youth ministry. Since my first day as a youth pastor I have always separated high school and middle school ministries. Even in the early years of running crazy small numbers, having minimal leaders, being part-time over two ministries, and even being portable, I have always done them separately! But if you have a smaller church and you are the only part-time or full-time youth staff, I understand why you would do the two ministries together.

After multiple conversations with other youth pastors who combine ministries, here are the main reasons I've discovered that churches combine ages:

♦ *Momentum*

One of the reasons churches combine their middle and high school ministries is the notion that bigger numbers equal momentum. Look, I understand what it can be like to lead a service or meeting with a really small group of students. But do the numbers really affect momentum? Do the numbers in our services really make that much of a difference to students, or is it more about stroking our own egos? I recently spoke to a church that was combining middle school through college in one service. In that service they were running about a thousand people. When I asked about the breakdown of students, what I found out was interesting, but not surprising. Seven hundred and fifty of the students were in college. About 150 or 200 were in high school, and about 50 to 100 were in middle school. So really they were doing a college service and inviting high school and middle school students to be a part of it. I am not trying to slam anyone for combining ministries; I just think we need to be intentional about how we do ministry. And if we are going to do something, let's be real about the reasons we are doing it.

A few years into doing youth ministry, I was under a lot of pressure for more numbers in our high school service, some from leadership and some self-imposed. I think we often put pressure on ourselves and become so focused on how many students are attending that we neglect to put into practice the very things that will bring those numbers. In the early years I would challenge students to bring friends (trying to shift that pressure to them); I would do big events and giveaways for students who brought the most. That didn't work. I remember being in a high school service one Sunday night and looking around at all the empty seats. In fact, it got to the point where I was more focused on the students who weren't there than the ones who were. I remember that one night God spoke to me clear as a bell and asked me, "Will you be faithful with what I've given you?" At that moment I decided that whether one or one thousand students showed up I would give it my best. This moment forever changed the way I approached youth ministry.

Let's get real for a second. I have often thought, "We need more students attending" or "When I plug these numbers into our weekly attendance it's not going to look good," but if I am being really honest, in over sixteen years of leading students I have never once heard a student say, "Man, I wish more students would attend" or "I am not coming back because it's too small." But I have heard the opposite, things like, "It's too big" or "I wish we could go back to it being small again." It's interesting that if we will just be honest with ourselves, sometimes we are the ones obsessing about attendance at a given event. And maybe, just maybe, our students don't really care? I have over the years seen parents get frustrated when we've done an event with middle and high school students combined. I have heard parents say they won't bring their young students because they don't want them hanging out with students who are that much older. And I have heard even more from high school students who don't want to be a part of an event or service with middle school students.

I have never in all my years in student ministry heard a student say, "I really wish we could combine middle and high school students so the group would appear bigger," as if magically more students would start coming if we did that. In actuality fewer students will come. You may have a larger single event or service, but the actual number of students engaged will decrease.

♦ *Cultural Shift*

We live in a different world now. Students are being exposed to more than they ever have before, at younger ages than ever before. This cultural shift is a reason for churches to combine student ministries. The argument is that middle school students are now facing many of the very same pressures that high school students are facing. Truth is...they are! I have been primarily working with middle school students for the last few years, and I will say that issues such as cutting, anxiety, depression, pornography, sex, drugs, and alcohol are all becoming more prevalent among middle school students. I understand the push to combine the two ministries, but the reality is that while the two groups might be facing some of the same issues, they handle them very differently. Emotionally, physically, and developmentally, middle school and high school students are different. There are some things you can say to a group of high school students that you shouldn't say to a group of middle school students. The way we communicate to high school students about sex and purity, for example, should be different from how we communicate to middle school students. If it's not, I am either doing high school students an injustice or ticking off the parents of our middle school students and potentially losing families from our church.

Equally Important

I am going to take slight rabbit trail here and point out that a lot of youth pastors tend to focus more of their attention on high school students—most likely because it's easier to connect with high school students and maybe middle schoolers seem intimidating or awkward. Look, I get it! I remember thinking early on that I would do both ages, and then, when the group got big enough, I would hand the middle school ministry off to someone else and focus on high school. It actually ended up happening the opposite way.

I am sure we all have stories of interactions with middle school students. A few come to mind for me. Like the time we were on a missions trip and were sitting around at the end of the day sharing how the day has affected us. (You know, one of those awesome youth ministry moments.) All of a sudden the attention quickly shifted to the corner, where one of our students was picking his toenails with his teeth. And the moment was gone! Sadly, this wasn't even the grossest thing this kid did on the trip.

And there was the time we took students on a ski trip and one of them determined that even though he was a Florida boy who had never been skiing before, he was somehow ready for a double black diamond. He ended up breaking his arm on the first day of the trip, which required me to spend the whole day with him at the hospital. Or—last one, I promise! I could write a whole chapter of these stories—I remember the time we were on a middle school retreat and one of the boys broke out a marionette (for my young readers, this is a doll on a string) and he continued to play with it all weekend. And then I had to explain to him why other kids were making fun of him.

Middle school ministry is crazy, awkward, and different, but I wouldn't have traded it for anything! Once I got past myself (because let's be honest, it's usually we, not the students, who are our biggest challenge) I soon discovered that middle school ministry is incredibly rewarding and meaningful. If you are starting a church or are new in your role as a youth pastor, I want to encourage you to start building the middle school students now, because if you do, in a couple of years they will be the core of your high school ministry. Just because students are experiencing more at a younger age doesn't mean they require the same approach.

♦ *It's Easier*

Drumroll, please! Here is, I believe, the main reason so many churches are choosing to combine their student ministries. A lot of youth pastors are volunteers or work part-time, and I get why it makes sense for you to combine ministries. Even if you're full-time it can be challenging to run multiple ministries. When I first started out in youth ministry, I was part-time. And when I say part-time, I mean really part-time! I was working multiple jobs to support my ministry habit. I was wearing multiple hats and doing everything from youth to kids to outreach to custodial to…You get the idea! Not to mention that we were portable for the first seven and half years of the church's existence. Every weekend we would transform a school into a church and then back into a school. Maybe you can relate to this, but if you have never been part of a start-up church, I'll tell you, it can be quite the experience!

I remember the days of getting to the elementary school at five in the morning. We'd do our best to make the main auditorium (aka the lunch room) feel less like a place where students ate their lunches and spread their germs and more like a place of worship. Then it was on to our youth auditorium (which was really a classroom that usually changed each week). We would do our best to cover the art projects, maps, and alphabet letters. Move all the desks to one side of the room and try to make it feel like a cool space for our students. This was just for our middle school service, and we would do a similar process for our high school students on Sunday night.

There were times when I wanted to combine ministries mainly because it would be easier on me. But something valuable I learned early on from my lead pastor is that "ministry isn't about what's easiest for us, but what's best for the people." This has altered the way I do ministry. How often do we make choices about our services, events, structures, programs, etc., because of what's easier for us, never really asking if it's what's best for the people we are leading?

I believe that separating student ministries is the best thing for the students we are leading. And often we make the choice to combine because we think we will gain momentum, because of cultural shifts, or honestly because it's just easier. Let me tackle a couple of the potential problems with combining ministries.

Middle school and high school students are different, and ultimately most churches offer a high school service and invite middle school students to come and be a part of something that's not really tailored for them. And unfortunately, our middle school students are the ones who miss out. They are treated like second-class citizens, when, to be honest, middle school is a huge time in a student's life, and sadly a lot of churches don't invest in students at an age when they are very moldable and are shaping their beliefs for the rest of their lives. Doesn't it make more sense to invest in students in middle school instead of hoping to grab them later, while they're in high school or college?

Another thing that I think gets overlooked is the whole parent dynamic. If I am the parent of a sixth-grade girl, there is no way in the world I am letting her come and hang out with some guys who are juniors and seniors in high school. I recently spoke to a youth pastor friend who decided to combine the two ministries, but after a year of doing it that way, he is now going back to separate ministries because he found that parents struggled with the idea of their middle school students being with high school students. He also discovered that most high school students didn't want to hang out with middle school students. In our services we are trying to reach the lost and unchurched, which is great, but keep in mind that having an innocent middle school student in the room with a lost high school student can create parental conflict and a variety of other issues. If you make the choice to combine the two age groups long-term, make sure that you and your church will be OK with the end results. And unless you are the exception and not the rule, your student ministry will primarily involve students in eighth through tenth grade. The older high school students will disengage, and the vast majority of your younger middle school or junior high students will not be allowed to come.

I think you have to decide what is best in the environment and culture you're in. And if you are smaller, you might have to make the choice to combine for a season or consider doing small groups rather than services until you see significant growth.

Just be willing to look at your student ministry and ask, "Why am I combining ministries? Is it really what's best for my students or just what's easiest for me.

3
Intentional Philosophy

What you believe determines the direction you take. That's why I believe that a youth ministry philosophy is essential to a healthy and thriving student ministry. What you do as a student ministry doesn't matter if you don't know why you are doing it, and one of the things I communicate to my team is that we can always change the *method* as long as we are still accomplishing the *why* behind it. I have learned over the years that I can't always carbon-copy what works in one culture and make it work in another. But I do believe that some principles transcend all cultures. In order to learn methods from others, you first must have a philosophy of your own. Just to be clear, I am not speaking about a purpose statement for your student ministry. I think we often spend too much time trying to create our own purpose or vision statements when in reality we should be in alignment with our church's vision and purpose statement.

How do we really gauge success? How do we know if what we are doing is working? Years ago I had a mentor who was pretty intentional about gauging the health of student ministry, and over the years I've developed a similar measure. I call it the *25-50-25 principle*. This principle or philosophy is the lens I use to look at everything we do as a student ministry. The idea is simply this: a healthy student ministry is composed of the following:

25 percent seeking

You promote an event that sounds fun (taco night, white out, color clash, or some other trendy-sounding event). Students show up, but before you ever get to the fun event that you promoted, you start with a thirty-minute worship set. Halfway through it, a handful of students who came with a friend get up and walk out. This isn't what they signed up for. Now you've missed an opportunity to connect with these students where they are, and your credibility is lost with the students who brought them, because they thought they were inviting them to something different. Trust me, I've been there! This is really what started to shift my thinking and where this principle was really birthed.

This group is most likely unchurched or new to church. They are seeking, searching, just checking out the whole God thing. This is essential to a healthy student ministry, because without them we become one-dimensional and often become deep without going wide. They are important to our churches and ministries because God has called us to reach the lost, hurting, and broken. Our tendency is to create services and events for our Christian students, usually with little thought to the unchurched student walking into the room. Maybe this looks or sounds different in your context, but I want to encourage you to make sure that you are being intentional about creating spaces that are conducive to reaching unchurched students.

What if we started to think this way and train our teams to think this way? How many students could we reach if we simply changed our approach?

50 percent growing

In Matthew 28, Jesus leaves us with this charge: "Go into all the world and make disciples of all men." I am a pastor at heart! I have always believed that if we are not taking our students somewhere, then what's the point? This is probably why for me the *seeking* students have required more of an effort. But maybe you tend to be more outreach minded and struggle with the discipleship side? Whether this is a strength or a weakness for you, you have to make sure you are being intentional about students' growth. These are the students who are growing in their faith. They are getting engaged beyond just attending a service. In our culture that means they have taken steps beyond attending a youth service. Steps such as participating in our growth track, small groups, camps, serving, outreach, etc.

25 percent mature

Hopefully it's obvious that when I say mature, I mean as mature as a student can be! These students are your core or maybe your student leaders. They are mature (for students) and understand that they are a part of something bigger than themselves. I can't stress how important it is that we are taking the students we've been entrusted with and intentionally developing them as leaders. This will create exponential growth in your ministry, but you are also creating a pipeline for the future.

I was recently in Japan, where roughly one-half of 1 percent of the population are Christians. As I started to learn more about the reason for this, it reconfirmed why developing students is such an important part of what we all do. Apparently there was a huge revival after WWII, missionaries flooded in, and nearly a third of the country gave their lives to Christ, which is why there are over seven thousand churches in Japan to this day. Sadly, they are nearly empty, and the people who are there are gray haired. They neglected to reach the younger generations, and as a result Japan is a very lost and hurting place.

Students will surprise you if you give them the chance. They can lead their peers and make a great impact for the kingdom of God. I am so grateful that over the years I've been under pastors and leaders who have believed in and empowered young people. What could happen in your ministry and church if you started to believe in and intentionally empower students in leadership?

Philosophy Phase Two

We've talked about what a healthy student ministry breakdown could look like, but how do we accomplish it? There is a second phase to the 25-50-25 principle. The first phase is really about gauging the health of your ministry. This phase will help you develop it. Every service, event, program, or ministry should exist to reach students who are seeking, growing, or mature. Some crossover will always happen, but these three main elements should always remain intact, in order to accomplish their purpose.

25 percent fun

Over the years I have been a part of ministries that were all about having fun. And while I am not here to criticize ministries built on this premise, I do struggle with this philosophy of youth ministry. You might very well go wide in your reach, but you will never go deep. Are we called to pastor and disciple students or just to be event planners who exist to fill students' social calendars? That said, I do want to stress the importance of having fun in your student ministries. Church and following Jesus should be fun, especially in the teen years! I encourage having a fun element in just about every ministry program, service, or event. And some things you offer students should be primarily fun, like services and outreach events. These two live in the fun column because we want these to be spaces where unchurched students can come and want to come back. It is important to note that our services will always have a relational and spiritual element as well.

I want to encourage you think outside the box! Over the years we implemented some programming that helped us to accomplish fun and outreach-minded experiences.

Once a month in our middle school service space we would do a fun event. No service element at all! No worship or message, just a really cool, fun event. We used this as a way to encourage students to invite their friends to a church event that wouldn't feel like a church event. Maybe some of you struggle with this idea; all I can tell you is that it got unchurched students there. And when it was done right, they came back. And when they came back, we had an opportunity to build a relationship with them and, more importantly, get them into a relationship with God.

50 percent relational

Life change happens in the context of relationships. This statement is vital when it comes to developing a healthy student ministry. To expound for just a second, you could say that life change happens in the context of four relationships. Clearly we all need and should be pointing students to a healthy relationship with God. But we also need to create spaces where students can connect with *mentors, peers,* and *mentees*. Below you will see what ministries live in the relational column to help us foster these three relationships.

◊ Groups

◊ Discipleship/growth track

◊ Serving

◊ Conferences

◊ Camps

◊ Missions trips

If our goal is that 50 percent of our students be growing, we need to make sure we have created adequate next steps for them to take in their growth process. When you have these next steps in place, you can start to address the next focus area.

<u>25 percent Spiritual</u>
Our goal should be to help take lost and unchurched students from that place to a place of spiritual maturity. So we have to offer opportunities for them to grow spiritually. Some of the things that primarily live in our fun or relational columns also have a spiritual element. I am sure that right now some of you might be concerned that I am saying only 25 percent spiritual. Here is the

reason I say this. I grew up in a student ministry that was primarily focused on the spiritual. Again, I am not here to criticize this way of doing ministry; in fact, that ministry and the leaders who invested in me are a big part of why I am who I am and where I am today. However, my youth group was the epitome of deep and not wide. We grew in our relationship with God and were given a great spiritual foundation, but we never really reached the lost and unchurched students, because our ministry was just not built with those students in mind.

Here are a few areas of ministry where you might try to help guide students into spiritual maturity:

◊ Student leadership
◊ Student coaching
◊ Internships

Once you have a philosophy of youth ministry, it should help to keep everything you do in its proper lane. To give you an example, there was a season when our high school services had become pretty deep, and it was as if we had forgotten that they were supposed to be a place to reach the 25 percent of students who were lost and seeking. When I met with some of our youth pastors, they explained that it was because they felt we weren't doing a great job of making disciples. They felt this healthy pressure to take students somewhere. We were just trying to accomplish it in the context of our services, and as a result we got to a place where our services were no longer accomplishing what they were created to accomplish. The beautiful thing that came out of this season was that we created more next steps for students so they could grow outside of our services. As a result we got our services back on track. Instead of having services that felt completely tailored to churched kids, our ministry again became a place where students who were lost, searching, and seeking could come and connect with what we were offering. I will expound more on what such services look like a little bit later.

Once you have a philosophy of youth ministry in place, you can start to take a look at each area of ministry you offer and evaluate its effectiveness. If you try to evaluate and make changes without having a philosophy of ministry, you will inevitably create chaos in your student ministries.

4

Intentional Experiences

If we are going to effectively reach students, we need to make sure that the experiences we create for them are executed with intentionality and excellence. I know there can be a lot of pressure on you as a youth pastor or leader to reach students. Your lead pastor wants you to meet with more parents. You have parents who are always on you to do more trips and events. The church up the street does small groups very successfully, and you feel you should do the same thing.

The guy at the youth conference said that the best way to reach students is to be super creative, and you want to be, but some of your students have an allowance bigger than your budget. (Can I get an amen?) So how in the world are you supposed to be intentional and create excellence in your youth environments?

I've learned a couple of things over the last sixteen years of doing student ministry. The first is not to add anything new until you can do it with excellence. Sometimes less is more! If your youth service isn't operating with some level of excellence, why add another event or program? If it's like pulling teeth to get students involved in local outreach, don't try to take them on a missions trip. If students aren't showing up for your small groups, why would you want to try to start after-school clubs? If you were to look at the programming I have set up within our student ministries, most of you would probably think, "How in the world do you keep all of that going, and with excellence?" The truth is, you don't want to add anything until excellence is achieved in the programs, trips, events, and services you're currently doing.

The second thing I learned was not to get caught up in what others expect. God called you to the ministry, right? So you ultimately answer to God. Obviously you need to respect and honor your leaders. But you need to know what God has called you to do and do it! If I tried to please every parent, pastor, and staff member in my church, I would never accomplish anything with excellence.

Let's dive a little bit more into the practical side of our services and experiences. Have you ever really looked at what you're doing and asked if it's intentionally reaching your target audience? This is huge if you are going to effectively reach the students God has called you to reach. Good intentions aren't enough. I believe every pastor and leader reading this book has good intentions. You want to reach students and affect their lives for Christ. But just because you have the desire to do that doesn't mean that you've been effectively doing it or that you even have the tools and resources to follow through with those desires. I am going to assume that within your service environment, for the most part you all have similar dynamics. So let's take a look at the service dynamics and find out just how intentional you are with each element of your service.

Environment

Every environment communicates something. If I tell you about a shopping experience I had recently at a large retail store, but don't tell you the name, I bet you could figure it out based on the details of my experience. So let's give it a shot. The other day I walked into a store to buy some supplies for my home, but when I finally found the area where you would expect to find these items, they were nowhere in sight, Not only could I not see them, I couldn't even find anyone to help me locate them. After several minutes of looking I finally found them in totally different area. So I finally made my way to the front of the store to make my purchase, and out of the fifty registers across the front of the store, a grand total of two were operating. So I waited in line for about twenty minutes, and when I finally got up to the register and said hello, the woman working the register appeared as if she hated life, and wasn't too concerned with my experience as a customer. So I exited the store, only to have employees stop me and check my receipt to make sure I hadn't stolen anything. I am guessing about halfway through my story you were able to guess what store I was referring to. Every environment communicates something! What are your environments communicating to the students who are walking into them?

I think we often associate the quality of our environment with the size of our budget. I remember being part of launching a church; in those days my budget was almost nonexistent, and we were a portable church. And this was before portable churches were a thing. We didn't have all the incredible resources that are at our disposal today. We met in an elementary school, so every weekend we had the daunting task of transforming a classroom into a cool youth environment. Actually, for our middle school service we literally shifted around from classrooms to libraries and even to portables located behind the school. And we had to accomplish this on a very limited budget. I used to think I was limited by the budget and space I had to work with, but the reality is that environment isn't solely about space or budget, but also about the atmosphere you create.

No doubt we all dream about the perfect youth space…stages, lights, LED screens, arcades, cafés, and I always envisioned a skate park. (Which, BTW, got shot down pretty quick. Something about insurance and student safety.) But the most important questions to ask about your youth environments are, "Do students feel welcome when they walk into the space?" "Do my leaders do a good job of connecting with students?" "Do they do a good job of connecting students to other students?" "Have you defined spaces in your environment to help get students connected?" "Are the lighting, decor, and music welcoming?" You can create a welcoming and engaging space without a massive budget. Just tap into your creativity and the creativity of your team.

Worship

There are many facets to the worship experience, so I want to break it down into a few areas that I think are really important and, honestly, where most of us miss it.

◊ *Quality*

I know that some of you might be in a church environment where the worship philosophy is "Let's just let the Holy Spirit do His thing." While I agree that we should not get in the way of the Holy Spirit moving and ministering to students, at what point did that become an excuse for us to not practice, to put people onstage prematurely, to put people onstage who should never be on the stage in the first place, and in general to have a worship experience that really wouldn't even qualify as a "joyful noise" to anyone? The worship experience exists to accomplish a couple of things. The first is to worship and connect with God; now, given that God is a God of order and excellence, why would we ever want to approach His throne offering anything less than our best? Second, worship exists to help the students in your ministry connect with God. If the music and worship element of your service is so bad that it actually distracts students from connecting with God, isn't that counterproductive?

Third, worship and music in our service should be a medium for attracting the lost and unchurched, right? Again, if a student walks in for the first time and the band sounds like karaoke gone bad, there is a good chance that they will never set foot back into your church—or any other church, for that matter.

Listen, I am all about getting students on the stage to lead. In fact, a few years ago we did something kind of revolutionary that might seem crazy to some of you. We decided to start a middle school worship band! I know, we were insane, right? Trust me, I second-guessed myself a lot of times, but truth is, it ended up being a huge win for us. There was a learning curve, but now we have a thriving middle school worship team made up of middle school and high school students. The important thing to remember is that quality does matter, and your youth service shouldn't be the training ground for just anyone who wants a shot at singing or playing an instrument. I want to encourage you to find a balance between creating opportunity for young musicians and vocalists and still maintaining excellence. Remember that excellence isn't about perfection; it's about doing the best with what you have.

◊ *Words*

OK, so I am standing in our youth service, and all of a sudden I find myself singing words about the "blood of the lamb who was slain." Being a guy who grew up in church, normally I wouldn't have thought twice about that, but I got to thinking, "Do the students in this service have any idea what that even means?" Or are they freaked out a little bit right now because they think God is into killing baby sheep? After service I approached members of our student worship team and asked them what those lyrics were referring to. To my surprise only one student (homeschoolers represent) was even close to being right. If we are going to create intentional worship experiences, shouldn't we make sure that we aren't using songs full of churchy lingo that students don't even understand? I want to refer back for a moment to the 25-50-25 principle. I spoke about how it's important to know the win so that we keep the focus in the right place. Worship is one of those things that spans the whole spectrum of students. Music is a universal language, and I believe worship is a great way for *seeking* students to connect. At the same time any student who is *growing* in their walk with God should be growing in their personal worship experience. And all of our students who are *mature* should be the ones leading the charge in our worship environments. Here is what I have discovered over the years: I have never seen a student who is mature in their walk with God be unable to worship because the words of a song were too simple. However, I have seen new or unchurched students who struggled with worship because the words were too deep or churchy. Even if you believe you are tone-deaf and have no musical ability at all, you need to be the one leading the charge and casting the vision for what worship will look like in your ministry area!

◊ *Audience*

I love worship! For me personally it is the best way to connect with God. If I were planning a worship service according to what I enjoy, I would probably do thirty to forty minutes of worship every service. However, it's not about what's best for me. It's about what's best for the students I've been called to reach. When we are planning the worship portion of our services, are we planning with our target audience in mind? If I am doing a middle school worship service, I am probably going to do about three songs and make sure that most of them are up-tempo. If I am at a retreat with high school leaders I might do extended slow worship. The key is being intentional with our worship experiences and taking our audience into consideration when we are planning worship services for them.

◊ *Training*

So maybe this will sound as if I am contradicting myself, given my strong stance on quality, but I believe it is possible to train and equip the next generation of worship leaders without sacrificing the quality of the worship experience. I think it's relatively common for high school ministries to have some form of a youth worship team, but a lot of student ministries are getting away from doing services, thus eliminating an ideal environment for developing the next generation of worship leaders. What I haven't seen is the intentionality of developing and creating this culture of worship from a young age. About six years into doing youth ministry I had what many of you might think was a harebrained idea—to be honest, so did I at the time. I now know it was totally from God. I wanted to develop young worshippers and help create a culture of worship in our middle school ministry, which at the time was nonexistent. Along with the help of our worship pastor we began auditioning middle school students for a band. To say it was rough at the beginning would be a gross understatement. At this point we were just looking for warm bodies who had even the slightest inkling of musical ability. And honestly, that's what we got! We had kids showing up and auditioning who had never sung or had a music lesson, and even students showing up with orchestra instruments, I still remember having to explain to one student that I didn't think the tuba would be a great fit for the worship team!

    What I will tell you is that some things are worth the pain in the beginning when compared with the outcome. Sometimes God gives you a vision for something that seems impossible. Sometimes you and I just need to be willing to create the culture. This can be a lengthy and hard process. As I look back at the decision, I can honestly tell you that it was definitely worth it! Not only did we create a culture of worship in our student ministries, we also created a culture where middle school and high school students were leading their peers in worship at a higher caliber than I've seen at most churches' main worship services. Some of those very students have now grown up and been hired at our church and others as worship leaders and pastors. While I will argue that quality is vital, sometimes you have to be willing to let that quality dip for a season to accomplish something greater.

Worship, when built and executed with intentionality, can set the tone in our student ministry. Worship really can be the element of our service or event that connects students with God and opens their hearts to be receptive to the truth that will be presented to them.

Communicators

You're watching an episode of *American Idol* when out comes a kid who thinks he can sing because that's what his parents have been telling him his whole life. As soon as he opens his mouth it becomes very apparent to the judges, everyone at home, and everyone anywhere within the sound of his voice that his parents have been building false hope. He is not a good singer and should never, ever have a microphone in his hand ever!

I think there is a valuable lesson to be learned here about who we have communicating in our churches and ministries. Sometimes we are too quick to hand off the microphone to someone who isn't ready or to someone who will never be ready. Look, a lot of people like to talk, but that doesn't make them good communicators. A person you put on stage to communicate—as a main speaker, as an emcee, or really in any capacity—should be someone qualified to speak. That might sound obvious, but sometimes we neglect the obvious. Any time you give someone a microphone, you are giving them a lot of control in your environment. Communicators can ignite an audience or kill it. They can engage and inspire or bore and turn off. If we are going to have intentional environments effectively reaching the very students God has called us to pastor, than we need to be very intentional about whom we have communicating in our services and at our events.

 Several years ago I gave one of my volunteer leaders an opportunity to preach in our middle school services. At the time we were doing four services a weekend. The first service started, and minus a few nerves at the beginning he was doing a pretty good job. The content was accurate. The delivery was decent. He then decided to do an illustration, which, being a very illustrative communicator, I loved! So I was sitting in the back of the youth auditorium and I saw him call up students for an illustration that we've probably all seen and most of us have done at some point. You have someone stand on a chair and someone else on the floor. The one on the chair tries to pull the other up and then the one on the ground tries to pull the other down. The takeaway is that it's easier to be pulled down than to lift others up. You know, a friends/whom-you-surround-yourself-with message.

So, this volunteer called up a boy and a girl. But what he didn't seem to notice was that the girl he called up was in a skirt and low-cut top. And of course he put the girl up on the chair, and all I can say is, it got awkward quick! So post-service I coached him on making sure he was aware of what students were wearing to prevent this from happening again.

The second service started, and again all was going well. So he decided that instead of calling up any girls he would play it safe and call up two guys. But for some reason he decided to have the guy on the chair sit on his knees instead of standing—to make it harder, I guess? The problem was that now the position of the kid's face who was standing did NOT look appropriate in relation to the other kid! Again I coached him on how the illustration should look.

The third service started, and the same scenario played out. Illustration time was upon us and I was in the back silently praying that he had this figured out by now. He calls up two girls; one is Caucasian and one is African-American. He then goes through the illustration but during it he looks at the white girl and says, "You represent the light" and, you guessed it...looks at the other girl and says, "You represent the darkness." At this point I was sitting in the back, face in my hands, literally contemplating if I should just quit the church and no longer try to pastor students. The good news is that by the last service of the weekend, the illustration went off without any hitches. The situation had been just as much my fault as his, because I should've done a better job of setting him up for success before he ever set foot on that platform.

We should always be identifying those around us whom we can help develop as communicators, but remember that there has to be something there to start with. One thing I have done over the years with potential communicators is to give them opportunities at smaller venues. For example, I would never have someone speak in our youth service until I've heard them speak at a small group or leaders event. If I have a first-time person emceeing, I pair them with an experienced emcee or myself to avoid any awkward moments. It really just comes down to being more intentional with how we develop communicators. Not only is giving someone an opportunity they're not ready for bad for the environment as a whole, but it can be a really negative experience for that individual as well. The best way I have found is not only to create smaller platforms where people can get some experience, but then to intentionally coach them as communicators. Take notes when they speak and give them practical advice that will help them grow in their skill set.

Message

We spoke about whom we choose to communicate, but equally important is what they are saying and how they are saying it. We live in a media-driven culture. Students are used to being entertained all the time with TV, movies, video games, phones, and the internet, just to name a few. And then we wonder why we can't keep students engaged in our messages. The truth is, a lot of the time we aren't speaking to students with intentionality. Honestly, even if you're a gifted communicator, you can still be teaching and preaching messages that are not intentional and are really missing the mark. I remember starting out in youth ministry; my goal was to be able to share a scripture and get students to laugh or cry. But there was no real intentionality in my messages. So how do we make the transition into effectively communicating to students in a way that is most relevant to them right now, in this season of their life?

◊ *Focus*

I used to just preach about whatever I wanted, and I honestly thought I could take any scripture about any subject and make it relevant to students. Look, you might be able to do just that, but is it the most relevant thing for your target age? Something we started doing a few years ago (I actually first heard about this concept while visiting North Point Church) was taking a look at our target age.

In my case it was middle school students. And I started asking, "What are the most relevant issues they are facing during their middle school years?" From that question my team and I came up with several topics we saw as being the most relevant to middle school students. As a result we have certain topics we hit every year, and if they don't fall within these perimeters we won't teach or preach them. The truth is that there are a lot of topics I could make somewhat relevant to middle school or high school students, but are they the *most* relevant to my target age group? It's so important that we stay focused and be intentional with what we are speaking about with our students.

Trendy doesn't always equal relevant

◊ *Creativity*

I used to equate creativity and money. I would think to myself, "Must be nice to have a big-enough budget that you can be creative!"

The reality is that creative messages aren't a direct result of the size of your budget or staff. In fact, for my first seven and a half years as a youth pastor, our church was portable. We met in two different elementary schools over the course of that time. So our middle school ministry would meet in classrooms and portables that often changed from week to week. Nothing screams *awesome environment* like school desks for seats and watercolor paintings by six-year-olds plastered all over the walls! So for those of you who can relate to the challenge of being creative with a limited budget, staff, and meeting space, let me offer you some hope and some practical ways to make sure that your messages are creative.

The first thing we did was to start having creative planning meetings. We would take a small group of our volunteers from various age groups and backgrounds and get together to brainstorm about how we could creatively package a relevant message to students. I would strongly encourage you to start doing this if you don't already. To be honest, I never really used to think of myself as "creative," but as we started doing these meetings I found myself getting more and more creative. I think most of us know that it's important to make sure we are mixing relevant stories and illustrations into our message. But we have started doing some things that have really taken our messages to a whole new level. So let me take a minute to tell you about a couple of the things we have done creatively. The next few pages will give you an idea of how we have creatively packaged some of our series. Feel free to use these ideas, but more importantly, I hope they will spark creativity with your team.

Series #1: "Dates on a Plane"

Topic: Dating/purity

Length: Four weeks

Concept: We spoke on dating and purity and used all things having to do with flying, planes, and airports as our creative piece.

Environment:

- We set up our chairs to look like rows on a plane.
- Outlines looked like boarding passes.
- Female volunteers dressed like flight attendants.
- Flight attendants handed out airline snacks (actual mini snacks used by airlines).
- The playlist pre- and post-service was all songs about flying and planes.

Week 1: "Destination"

The premise of the message was this: You wouldn't get onto an airplane without knowing where it was going. Why would you jump into a dating relationship with someone when you have no idea where it is going?

Week 2: "Baggage"

The premise here was that dating the wrong way leads to baggage. Illustratively we had luggage all over the platform, and I used it during the message to illustrate that dating the wrong way will always lead to relationship baggage.

Week 3: "Standby"

Here the concept was waiting for God's best in our relationships. We spoke on being OK with being single, how some things in life are worth waiting for, and not rushing into dating relationships, but waiting for Gods best.

Week 4: "Terrorists"

The theme this week was things that will destroy relationships. We really focused on the importance of purity and how when you start crossing physical lines prematurely it can destroy your relationship and create serious issues in future relationships.

Series #2 "Mall Madness"

Topic: Dating/purity

Length: Four weeks

Concept: We spoke on dating and purity and used all things having to do with shopping, stores, and malls to communicate truths of dating.

Environment:

- We hung shopping bags from mall stores on walls.
- We did giveaways from those stores. (If you're operating with a limited budget, hit the clearance racks.)
- We gave away a shopping spree at a local mall at the end of the series.
- Pre- and post-service playlist songs were about relationships.

Week 1: "Window Shopping"

The concept this week was avoiding dating before you're ready. Instead of window shopping when you don't have any cash to spend, save up until you do. We used that to speak on becoming the right person now so that one day when you meet the right person you will have something to offer.

Week 2: "Fitting Room"

This week we had a clothes rack onstage with various shirts and a dressing room made from PVC pipe and fabric. I spoke about how most stores limit the number of items you can carry into the fitting room and used this to speak about limiting the dating relationships you're in.

Week 3: "Baggage"

As with the luggage message in the previous series, we had shopping bags all over the platform. I spoke on how sometimes we go shopping and come out with a lot more bags than we planned on. Then I spoke on limiting the baggage we pick up in our dating relationships.

Week 4: "Overspending"

I set up with a story about how I went shopping one day for a Christmas gift, but ended up spending a lot more than I planned on and came out with more stuff than I anticipated. Then I tied it in with how crossing physical boundaries in relationships will always cost you more than you realized.

Series #3 "Sweet Tooth"

Topic: Dating/purity

Length: Three weeks

Concept: We spoke on dating and purity and used all things having to do with candy to communicate dating truths.

Environment:

- Candy rap intro video.
- The café had various kinds of candy for sale.
- Each week we gave away candy corresponding to our message to every student as they left (mini/fun size).
- The playlist pre- and post-service was all songs about candy. (If you do this, check the lyrics first!)

Week 1: "Nerds"

The setup this week was about how our self-image affects our dating relationships. We spoke about seeing ourselves the way God does regardless of labels and things people have said about us.

Week 2: "M&M's"

We had multiple varieties of M&M's on stage and compared trying new flavors to jumping from relationship to relationship. We spoke on how important it is to limit the flavors we try. That God didn't design us to jump from dating relationship to dating relationship.

Week 3: "Conversation Hearts"

This week was leading up to Valentine's Day, so we used conversation hearts and spoke about being cautious about whom you give your heart to and the importance of protecting purity.

Series #4 "Drive"

Topic: Dating/purity

Length: Three weeks

Concept: We spoke on dating and purity and used all things having to do with cars and driving to communicate truths of dating.

Environment:
- Car parts from junkyards, gas cans, license plates, etc.
- Each week we had remote-controlled cars on a track we built.
- We drove a real car into the space. (We borrowed it from a local dealership.)
- Each week we gave away car-related stuff (air fresheners, key chains, *Cars* DVD, etc.).
- Pre and post-service playlist songs were about cars and driving.

Week 1: "Car Model"

The premise is that God made you a Ferrari, not a Focus. We used this to speak on self-worth and not settling for less than God's best in your relationships. I actually started this message from inside a car that we drove into our youth space.

Week 2: "GPS"

I kicked this week off with a story about getting lost while driving. Then I talked about GPS and how to date with purpose.

Week 3: "Mudding"

I set up with the statement that "Ferraris aren't designed to go mudding." Then I tied that in with a message of purity and that God designed you for something better than what most people experience. At the end of the message I gave each student a Hot Wheels car.

These are just a few of the series we have done over the years. As you can see, they all focus on a topic very relevant to our target age; we just packaged them differently. I believe that students connect, engage, and ultimately remember the words we say when we make them sticky. I know some of you may be thinking, "The Bible is enough" or "Truth is enough." Why do we need to package it in some creative/sticky way? Jesus did! Think about it: He always spoke in parables so that the average person of the day could understand what He was talking about, contrary to the belief of some that He did it to confuse people. The only people He confused were the religious leaders who were out of touch with the common man. Let's make sure we are communicating truth in a creative and relevant way that is in touch with the common student God has called us to reach.

Flow

We have all been in a service before where the flow wasn't working and it really killed or at least hurt the dynamics of the service. So let's take a look at this aspect of our service environments. The flow of your service or event is really kind of subjective, and I don't claim to know what works best for where you are at and who you are as a ministry. The beauty of flow is that it can work in many different ways. I don't think there is an exact science to having effective flow. What works for one church might not work for another. So how do we have intentional flow? I think it really comes down to trial and error and not being afraid to change our flow and experiment until we find what works best for us. I will say that transitions are really important! Something that has really helped us with our excellence in flow is to have a volunteer or staff person to coordinate your service. If you are the one hitting the lights, pressing play on the video, turning the lights back on, and running to the stage to speak, most likely there will be some rough transitions in your environment. We have also implemented a post-service review meeting. This meeting is with the key players in our services, such as the worship leader, service coordinator, sound/tech director, etc. There are also a couple of key leaders whom I have given the right to speak into my life as a communicator and give their opinions on my message. This way we can look at the flow of our service and make adjustments for future services.

> **Every environment communicates something. Make sure your environments are communicating what you want them to.**

I feel that this is an important place to pause and remind us all of something. I know that we have a hit a lot of practical steps and spoken about things you can do to improve the overall level of your ministry. I just want to remind you all that these things are just tools to help us more effectively reach and pastor students. Don't let your ministry become about the tools, systems, and structures. Just let those things help you do the ministry more effectively. OK, let's continue…

5

Intentional Growth

Let's talk about numbers. Some of you probably just cringed in your seat, because numbers are one of the things you hate talking about. Maybe because every time you get called into the lead pastor's office you have to answer the questions about attendance, and maybe you leave that meeting feeling like a failure because you don't have a thousand students coming to your youth service. Or because every time you get together with other youth pastors the question always comes up: "How many students are you running?" Maybe you have put pressure on yourself to grow, and because you aren't hitting the numbers you'd like or as many as the youth group around the corner, you feel like a failure. I am sorry if the mere title of this chapter causes you to stress out. But the truth is that numbers are important! The problem is that too often we measure success simply by the number of students attending our services, and that is not an accurate way of gauging a healthy and thriving student ministry. Numbers are important because numbers tell a story. However, it's not enough to just look at the number of students attending your service. For an accurate portrait of the health of your student ministry, you need to broaden your view. A large number of students attending a service is great! But a concert, a blockbuster, or a number of other events can have a large crowd show up, and it doesn't mean that any life change is happening. There are a few key areas that I believe we need to look at if we want to accurately view the health of our programs. Before we dive too far into each of these areas I want to encourage you to define what health looks like in your student ministry.

Services

We have all felt pressure from others and ourselves to increase attendance and grow our youth services. I remember in the early years of our high school service feeling those very pressures. It got to a point where I would stand in the back of the auditorium and stress out over the empty seats. I remember one night I was doing just that and I felt God asking me if I was going to be faithful with the students who were there or if I was going to keep worrying about the ones who weren't. That night was a catalyst moment for me. I made a choice to be faithful with what God had given me. To give it my all regardless of whether one hundred students showed up or three. Look, I absolutely believe that we should strive to have our services packed with students. Truth is, a lot of students are lost and need Jesus in their lives, and I want to reach as many of them as I can. But too often our tactics and strategies for getting them there don't work! I know from experience. Let's take a look at some of the common strategies used in our student ministries.

◊   *Pressure Shifting*

This is one of the least useful tactics. We have this pressure on us (sometimes self-imposed) to get more students to our services. So what we do is try to shift that pressure onto the students. We do a whole message or even series on sharing our faith, but really it's more about growing our service. So we try to make students feel the pressure to grow the student ministry. And the truth is that that never works. Because even though students should be inviting friends to the youth service, pressuring them to do so is pretty ineffective, because it's not a priority for them. I remember saying things like, "Your friends could end up in hell if you don't invite them to service" or "You are the only Jesus your friends might see." How many of you know that while these are accurate statements, getting students to be passionate about that cause isn't an easy task? So you can spend your time trying to make that a priority for them, but I can say from experience that that never seems to bring the results you are looking for.

◊ *Growth by Gimmick*

This is another popular strategy that usually produces very little fruit. Most of us have probably done this before: we have some special service or event, and in an effort to get students to bring their friends we offer something really cool like a brand-new iPad, money, or a video game system. This might get some new students there, but it won't keep them there. When I used to try this it never really worked. You'd always have maybe one kid who brought like ten friends, and no one else would bring anyone. So you end up spending your budget on something that really produces little to no fruit.

You can try to pressure students, you can try all the gimmicks, but if you want to see effective growth in your service environment, you need to work on creating a service experience that students want to invite their friends to. It doesn't matter what you give away or how much pressure you put on your students. When your services are relevant and excellent, and students love coming, they will invite their friends.

> **My experience has taught me that gimmicks, guilt, and giveaways simply don't work.**

◊ *Bait and Switch*

A group of students show up at the service that you promoted to your students as a fun event—maybe a Christmas party or a color clash, or maybe you're really trendy and do a silent DJ. These students have never been to your church before, but are giving it a try because a friend invited them on the premise that it wasn't going to be a church service, but a fun event. However, they show up to a church service and the fun event you promised is merely a short afterthought. I want to encourage you to be cautious of trying to build your ministry this way. Students will start to lose trust and will no longer invite their friends. And then when you do have a new or unchurched student show up, short of a miracle, they probably won't be back! Jesus tells us in Matthew chapter 5 to "Let your yes be yes and your no be no." Our words and our actions should match up. We need to be intentional with how we reach students in the context of our services, and we need to make sure that we are doing what we say we are going to do. This will add credibility and should create trust with your students so they can invite their friends without worrying about what they're going to experience when they show up.

Discipleship

Even if hundreds—or even thousands—of students show up for your youth service, if there is no discipleship happening, is your youth ministry truly healthy? God has called us to pastor students, and last time I checked my Bible, Jesus told us to "go into all the world and make disciples," not to go into all the world and have huge service experiences. So while our services are important and should be an environment for reaching the lost, what's the point if we aren't taking them somewhere? I think the real problem is that most of us don't have any real, intentional way to disciple young people. We hope that our leaders are helping to disciple them, but there is no real system in place to help with that process. I am part of a church network that believes that *life change happens in the context of relationships.* And while I wholeheartedly agree with this statement, I believe sometimes we become one-dimensional in our understanding of it. Life change does happen in the context of relationships, or a better way to say it would be, "Life change happens in the context of four relationships":

- o Relationship with God—I know this seems obvious, but I had to say it!

- o Relationships with peers—I think we do a good job of encouraging peer-level relationships. We talk about the importance of friends all the time! But two other relationships are essential in all our personal development.

- o Mentor relationships—We all need mentors and should be encouraging students to find theirs. Hopefully this relationship can happen in the context of your student ministry. This is one of the reasons a strong adult leader is important to the health of your ministry.

- o Mentee relationships—We should all have people in our lives whom we invest in and encourage students to do the same. A great way to encourage this is by developing a strong student leadership team.

When we have that understanding and we implement that into our student ministries, the natural occurrence is discipleship! I also want to encourage you as a youth pastor to always be making disciples of and pastoring your students. Even if you are a large church and you think "I will just have my leaders do it, because I have more important things to do"—NO YOU DON'T! Do for the *one* what you wish you could do for them all. And don't expect your leaders to do something that you aren't willing to do yourself!

If you want to know how healthy your student ministry is, stop gauging health solely on service attendance and start looking at other numbers. How many students have accepted Christ? How many students are being discipled? How many students are in small groups? How many students have gone on missions? How many students are becoming leaders? You see, all of these numbers are just as important in determining the health of your student ministry. In actuality they are more important. Don't deceive yourself by thinking that you are winning because you have a lot of students attending your service or event. Where are you taking them?

Leaders

I don't want to spend a whole lot of time here, as we will be covering "Intentional Leadership" in another chapter. However, if you're not growing leaders, any growth you think you are experiencing in your service environment is really just an illusion. Growth without growing leaders isn't sustainable. I have heard youth pastors talk about how they grew their ministries to thousands, but because they never focused on leaders it all fell apart. I have seen this firsthand. If your student ministry is built solely on your personality, what happens when you leave? And while I hope you are youth pastor for the long haul, you will leave at some point. True success is measured by your successors. And I don't care how dynamic a personality you have; without growing leaders and giving ministry away, your efforts are in vain. Build your ministry to last longer than you will. The most effective way to do this is to be a developer of leaders.

Outside the Church Walls

My lead pastor told me early on to pastor not just the students who come to our church, but the students in our community as well. I used to be at every school lunch, concert, and sporting event I could. As your ministry grows, the frequency with which you can attend events will probably change. The good news is that if you're intentional about your approach, you can have a great impact that goes beyond what you could ever do on your own. I have discovered that empowering students to do ministry on their campuses is a very effective way to reach other students. If you're like me, it breaks your heart that there are thousands of students in your community who are lost, hurting, and broken and have never experienced God's love in their lives. But the reality is that they are not all going to come to my youth service, or any church service, for that matter.

One of the things we did to try to expand our influence outside the four walls of the church was to start video campuses. We have done this effectively with our middle school ministry. We have had middle school video campuses involving multiple schools, seeing 150-plus students biweekly right on their school campuses, with nearly 70 percent of those students not even attending our church or youth ministry. If we are going to have intentional growth, it shouldn't be limited to what happens inside the walls of the church.

Numbers are important! Thousands of students in our communities don't know Christ, so we should absolutely pay attention to our numbers and focus on intentional growth. Let's just make sure we are intentional in growing healthy student ministries, not just big services!

6
Intentional Leadership

I won't take a lot of time to write about leadership principles in this chapter, because there are dozens of great leadership books out there. I really want to focus primarily on what has worked and not worked for us when it comes to next-generation leadership and empowering and producing leaders.

John Maxwell says it best: "Everything rises and falls on leadership."

The truth is that you can have all the other elements in place—relevant environments, great communicators, dynamic services, and events—but without an intentional focus on your personal leadership and the leadership of your team, none of that matters. So let's take a minute and talk about my next-generation leadership philosophy, and then we will get really practical with how that plays out in our student ministries.

Leadership Philosophy

My influence and impact as a leader are the direct results of how well I empower others. Maybe you are juggling multiple ministries in your church. Maybe you're working another job to support yourself and your family. Maybe you want to have a healthy, thriving student ministry, but you feel stretched to the max already. You can't do it all. Look, I've been there and know how it feels to be in those seasons. I remember feeling pressure to grow, wanting to accomplish more and reach more students for Christ, but not feeling as if I had any more capacity to accomplish that task. I wish that I had really valued the concept of empowering others when I first started out in youth ministry, but better late than never, I suppose.

If you want to have a healthy and thriving student ministry, you have to empower other leaders. However, I feel the need to say that empowering leaders doesn't mean just giving away the stuff you don't like doing. In fact, one of the greatest ways to empower leaders is to give away parts of the ministry you enjoy.

> **There is a significant difference in delegating tasks and empowering others to lead.**

If you hold on too tight to the reins of your student ministry, you will have a hard time keeping leaders, you will be frustrated with the influence of your ministry, and it will ultimately collapse from the inside out. This is hard for some of us because we are the leaders or the youth pastors, and honestly, sometimes we let pride keep us from really empowering the leaders around us. If you struggle with empowering leaders and feel threatened by other strong leaders around you, you are probably an insecure leader and need to deal with that before you hurt yourself and others.

I will never forget one night when one of my adult leaders asked me to come out and hang with him and the guys in his small group. I got there just before students started arriving, and one after another I saw students coming up to this leader and greeting him as "Pastor _____." To be perfectly honest, internally I struggled with it at first. I wanted to stop and correct them—after all, *I* was their pastor. But then it hit me: This was a huge win! At that moment I started to shift my focus and realized that the more I empowered leaders around me the greater my sphere of influence would be. Up to that point I had been small minded about our student ministries. When you hear what I am about to say, some of you will strongly disagree. So let me preface it by saying that this is seasonal.

In the early years I was at all the school lunches, every game, concert, youth event, and trip. I thought that to be effective I needed to be with the students constantly, but I was wrong. The truth is, I was being small minded, and until I shifted my focus I found myself at a plateau. Your time is better focused on developing leaders than it is being with students 24-7. I say this is seasonal because once you develop a core of leaders it actually allows you to spend more time with students. Also, a lot depends on the structure of your student ministry. I am part of a multisite church where we do video broadcasts out and handle the vast majority of the administrative responsibilities so people at each campus don't have to. As a result, the role of a youth pastor at a campus is primarily to execute services, raise leaders, and pastor students. I do think that sometimes the bigger our ministries grow the less we pastor students, but we will dig into that thought a little more later on.

Building Your Team

I want to speak to this for a moment, because I have heard and seen multiple student ministries that have this mind-set of "If they are over twenty-five years old they shouldn't be leading students." This is narrow-minded, foolish, and ultimately destructive to building a healthy student ministry. Some of the best leaders on my team over the years have been older than that. In fact, the majority of my leaders have been older than I. I think back to when I was a student and attending youth group; one of the single greatest influences in my life was a little German lady in her fifties. I wouldn't be the man or leader I am today without her influence in my life! She played a huge role in my spiritual development, faith, and prayer life. I am so grateful for her and for my youth pastor, who valued her regardless of age. I strongly believe that a healthy student ministry needs an adult leadership team and a student leadership team. They are both integral to developing a healthy student ministry, for two very different reasons. Adult leaders add stability, structure, and mentorship to your team. Not to mention that when they're developed and empowered the right way, you can start to hand ministry off to them, which creates more capacity for you. Student leaders, on the other hand, will bring growth to your student ministry numerically! When you empower students to lead, you are giving them ownership and buy-in to the student ministry. Also, you are training future leaders and pastors.

    I want to encourage you not to write off students, thinking they are too young or inexperienced to lead. If you give them a shot at it, you will be surprised at what they can accomplish and the value they can add to your student ministry and your church. I could share dozens of stories of students who have led beyond my expectation.

So I don't lose you, I will just share one. There was a student in our ministry who started coming in sixth grade. He was shy and slightly awkward, but he had a great heart. He became one of our student leaders, and at the start of his seventh grade year he became our first after-school club leader on his middle school campus. He continued to grow as a leader and communicator.

Today he is twenty years old and has led missions trips, led retreats, and spoken in front of hundreds of students. We ultimately hired him, and now he is off helping with a church plant across the country. Don't write off adult leaders on the grounds that they're too old, and please don't write off student leaders because you think they are too young. These are honestly two of the greatest misses in youth ministry. If you choose to operate this way, you will do your students a huge injustice. I will never forget a few years ago when I took a group of middle school student leaders on a missions trip to El Salvador. The youth pastor there was pretty successful in his own right. He was reaching hundreds of high school students. However, as our time with him came to an end, he shared with me that he had been inspired by the way these students led and did ministry.

That inspired him to start a middle school ministry at his church, which I guess is a pretty foreign concept in most churches across Central America. Trust me when I tell you from experience not to write people off because of their age.

I want to encourage you to be intentional with your leadership. We have access to so many great resources, from books to podcasts to conferences. As leaders we have to make sure first that we are growing in our own leadership and then that we are developing the leaders around us. I promise you that time spent developing leaders is never time wasted. God can use you to accomplish great things, but I am confident He doesn't plan for you to do it alone!

7
Intentional Discipleship

I know we briefly spoke about discipleship earlier, but I think this is a topic worth devoting a chapter to. If we are growing wide without growing deep, we are missing the mark. In Jesus's final words in the Gospel of Matthew, He charges us to "Go and make disciples"—not merely converts. As youth pastors and leaders, we need to be taking our students somewhere.

My fear is that we have become really good at gaining converts and selling the gospel, and that the result is students signing up to become Christian, but not necessarily to become disciples. I think this is probably because we haven't been intentional about the process. I think it's important for us to have a discipleship plan or track in place; I am a systems and structures guy. But the structure we have in place or the programming we use to disciple students can only be a tool to help in the process. True discipleship can't happen unless we build intentional relationships. By all means have a program! Have a structure or system to help disciple students! But it can't stop there. Discipleship happens when students get the opportunity to do life with someone.

My youth pastor was the single greatest influence in my life. I would not be where I am today or who I am today without his being intentional about discipleship and mentorship. He simply invited me to be part of his life. I spent time with him at his home; I saw how he treated his wife and kids. I saw how he interacted with others at church and while hanging out with him at his office. He included me in his life, and whether he did it on purpose or not, that's what discipleship is. Being a disciple is more caught than taught. Jesus chose twelve men and then invited them to be part of his life. That was the genius and intentionality of Jesus. Sometimes we try to overcomplicate or reinvent the wheel, when Jesus (the ultimate disciple maker) showed us how over two thousand years ago. If you have a large student ministry or desire to grow and reach more students, you will need to make sure you are empowering leaders around you to disciple students. Even if you're great at making disciples, your ceiling will be relatively low if you're not empowering others to do the same.

Structure

While discipleship happens through relationships, I believe you can be intentional about creating systems and programs to help facilitate the discipleship process. I personally realized that trying to take students through multiple weeks of classes wasn't going to be a win for us. I don't know about you, but in our culture that was like pulling teeth. So I had the idea to move from a classroom model to an experience model. A lot of churches I am connected with use some form of growth track programming. This concept is not new; I simply took what I saw in other cultures and started to ask, "How would this work best in our culture?" So we developed a growth track for our students, consisting not of classes spread out over multiple weeks, but of event-type experiences. I found that it was a lot more productive, and more students were engaging in the process than when we were trying to get them to attend a series of classes.

Here's what this approach has looked like in the culture I've been a part of:

Grow Weekend—An overnight event that covers the basics of being a Christ follower, such as salvation, water baptism, reading the Bible, prayer, worship, sharing faith, etc.

    - Small-group feel (usually capped at twenty).

    - Takes place in someone's home (more interactive).

    - Starts at 7:00 p.m. on a Friday and ends at noon on Saturday.

This has been a great way to teach the basics. Create a culture where the topics can be discussed and questions can be asked, and foster relationships with students and leaders.

Encounter Weekend—A weekend retreat designed to take students a little deeper. Students engage in worship, small groups, and services where we address the cross, purpose, generational and habitual sins, who the Holy Spirit is, etc.
- Takes place at a retreat center over a weekend.
- We start retreat night by showing *The Passion of the Christ*.
- Small groups throughout the weekend.
- Fun activities.

Going on this retreat has been a great way for students to experience freedom and gain a deeper understanding of the cross and who the Holy Spirit is, and again it fosters relationships with leaders and other students.

Motivation Day—A three-hour event designed to help students understand how God has gifted and wired them.
- Students take a spiritual gift/motivations test.
- Coaching on what the outcomes mean about them and their relationships, attitudes, and purpose.

This is really a great entryway into their understanding how they are wired and how to interact with others who are different.

Again, these are all just tools designed to help create a base and foster the relationships in which true discipleship happens.
I want to encourage you to be intentional about the discipleship process. Maybe creating a system like this (or using this one) will help you accomplish this. But at the end of the day it's about being there for students. Inviting them to be a part of your life. You don't have to create special events or things to do. If you're going shopping for an event, invite a student along. Have students to your home and let them hang with you and your family. Just let

them see how you live and allow them to be a part. Another way to accomplish this is to engage in their world. A student is playing in the football game Friday; show up and cheer them on! A student is singing in the spring chorus concert, go and watch! The kid who is a little country is showing their pig or cow at the fair, go and support them! The impact that kind of stuff has is way more significant than what happens for an hour and half on a Wednesday night or Sunday morning. Just do life with them and empower your leaders to do the same!

8
Intentional Evaluation

We are all familiar with "sacred cows" within the church. You know, the things we do and keep doing because they've always been done, even though no one can tell you why. Honestly, even if you are part of a young or relatively young church, you can already have some sacred cows. It really doesn't take long to create them within our ministries. They usually start out with a purpose or goal. They might have even really worked in your ministry at one point, but because no one ever evaluated them or asked the hard questions, they've kept going even though they no longer work. I have been involved in ministries that were at one point thriving and effective, but because they never asked the right questions and evaluated what they were doing, they became irrelevant.

Being relevant has become a cultural trend within the church. Some people hate that word because they think it implies a watering down or secularizing of the gospel. Truth is, being relevant was God's idea a couple thousand years ago. God looked at his creation, His laws, and His relationship with us, and saw that there needed to be some changes.

So He sent Jesus to this Earth in the ultimate act of relevance. You see, God Himself asked the hard questions and, when needed, made some changes to the way He related with humans. So Jesus came to the Earth, became human, and dwelled among men. All the while He exemplified relevance in His ministry from His messages to the way He connected with people. Being relevant shouldn't be thought of as something to avoid, but instead something we as leaders should embrace. If we are going to have sustained success we must have sustained relevance, and in order to have sustained relevance we must ask intentional questions. I know this can be a challenging thing for us as leaders because asking these kinds of questions might require change in our ministry and, even harder, change in ourselves. But if we neglect to ask hard questions we will never be able to have any kind of sustainable success.

Asking the right questions requires that you have intentional systems in place to properly evaluate the various areas of your ministry. Let me just tell you how this has played out within our student ministries over the years. We have created platforms to be able to effectively evaluate all our ministry areas.

Platform #1: Service Review

These review meetings have been very effective for us in evaluating our weekly youth services. If you have multiple services happening on the same weekend, a meeting allows you to make any necessary changes before the other services. But even if you are doing one service a week, having a review meeting while the service is still fresh will help you to do it better the next time. In these meetings we make sure to have all the key players in the room. For us that means we have our service producer, sound engineer, worship leader, and speaker in that meeting. You don't want to have too many people in this meeting, otherwise you won't accomplish much. We will actually walk through the service from start to finish and evaluate everything: pre-service, emcees, flow, cues, video and audio, lighting, worship, and the message. This helps us to make the changes needed so we can execute future services with a higher degree of excellence. In order for this to work you have to give permission for people to be real about the service (even the message).

Platform #2: Event Review
The main idea behind these reviews is to help us get better for the next time, whether it's a recurring event or not. Anytime we have an event, we like to have a review meeting while the event is fresh in our minds to evaluate all aspects of it. Possible changes, things we liked or didn't like. Really anything that would help the overall success of the event in the future. After some of our events we actually have feedback forms for students to fill out so we get their feedback as well. This has been a great tool for us in making sure that we are effectively accomplishing the purpose of the event.

Platform #3: Staff Reviews

We have monthly staff meetings, and in these meetings we make sure to evaluate services and events, but also to evaluate our coaches, leaders, structures, promotion, etc. This has been a very valuable practice for us. Even if you don't have a staff and you are working with volunteers, this will help to remove some of the pressure on you to try to make sure everything is operating as it should be. Often someone on the team will have a great idea, and you can let them roll with it. It gives them ownership and adds value to them as a leader while helping to accomplish something positive in your ministry.

Platform #4: Yearly Review

This has been absolutely, hands down, one of our biggest wins! We started doing a yearly review meeting several years ago, and it has paid huge dividends. This meeting is made up of staff and a small handful of high-level leaders in our ministry area. Again, you don't want to invite every volunteer or leader you have, because you would be there all night and get very little accomplished. This meeting is really all about looking over the past year at everything you have done.

- Programs
- Events
- Trips
- Services
- Series
- Missions
- Outreach
- Leadership teams

We literally take a look at everything we do as a ministry and evaluate it. Does it line up with our ministry vision? If it doesn't, we cut it from the next year's calendar. Was it successful? If it wasn't, even if it lined up with our vision, we ask, "How can we make it more successful?" If we don't feel we can make it more successful, we cut it.

Let me give you a personal example of this. We used to do a monthly memory verse within our middle school program, but the percentage of students participating was ridiculously small. I think it was something like 2% of our total attendance. It lined up with our vision, so we asked, "How can we get more participation?" So we tried to promote it better and really pushed it, but with the same results. At that point we decided that even though we believed that it was important and lined up with our vision, the participation wasn't worth the effort we were investing in it, so we cut it.

One of the things I do in this meeting is share percentages of involvement of our various programs, trips, and events, and compare them to those of the previous year. If we are seeing growth, we leave it alone. If we are staying the same or have less participation, we again ask the hard questions and determine if changes need to be made to that particular event, service, or program.

This has been a huge win for us, even though I will tell you as a leader that sometimes it hurts when something you birthed gets cut or is brought up as a failure. You have to be willing to receive honest feedback and criticism from your team. Actually, you have to give your team permission to be honest with you, or else these meetings won't accomplish anything. Some of the things we've cut from our program were things I came up with. Some of them had even been effective at one point, but they'd lost their relevance within our ministry, so I had to be willing to let go.

Platform #5 Self-Review

Evaluating yourself is probably the most difficult of all reviews or evaluations. I don't just mean in the context of a yearly employee review or however your church reviews you. I mean honest, hard, unbiased self-evaluation. Sometimes in ministry the people around us aren't honest with us. Sometimes when we ask for feedback it's only positive and about how great we are. That's one of the main reasons I believe that from time to time we need to take a good hard look at ourselves and ask the hard questions:

- ◊ Am I leading myself well?
- ◊ Am I leading others well?
- ◊ How is my relationship with God?

- ◊ Are my marriage and family healthy?
- ◊ Am I in the right seat on the bus?
- ◊ God, is this still the place you've called me to be?
- ◊ Whom am I developing?
- ◊ Am I effectively pastoring students?
- ◊ Is there any offense or heart issue in me?

You get the idea. It is so important that we find times to ask ourselves these questions. I find that I need to get away from everything for a couple of days. Just me and God alone, without any other distractions. This was challenging for me the first few times I did it, but the end result has been very healthy.

If we are going to have a healthy student ministry, we have to make sure we are asking intentional questions. We also have to make sure we are giving our teams or at least some people on our teams permission to ask intentional questions as well. This can't happen if we are insecure as leaders. If we have a problem letting other people challenge and ask the hard questions about our ministry, we might need to check our hearts. Because no matter how long we've been doing it or how good we might be, the truth is that we can always be better. But in order to be better we have to be intentional and ask intentional questions.

9
Intentional Structure

I know some of you saw the title of this chapter and are contemplating skipping it. I get it! For some, talking systems and structures isn't exciting. However, developing intentional structures will help you to lead and pastor students more effectively. Let me give you a few thoughts that might help you with structure.

The Why

First, you have to know what your ministry purpose and mission are. Once you have this, it will help you to develop your structure around your why. Systems and structures aren't the win. They should simply exist to help you win! A good personal example of this would be our student leadership team. Years ago I started to develop this team, but as it continued to grow we got to a point where I realized I couldn't effectively take care of all of our student leaders, let alone the students attending and our adult leaders as well. So a structure was born! I met with our team and started asking how we could take better care of our student leaders. The answer came in the form of a student leader coaching structure. Basically, from our pool of student leaders we identified some of the more mature students who had a little more capacity than others. We then met with them and rolled out our vision for the new structure. We assigned two or three of our student leaders to each student leader coach and explained that our heart was for the coaches to invest in the leaders and make sure they were doing life with these students. That meant weekly calls and texts and hanging out at least once a month. This was a huge win because it helped us to take better care of our students.

The win is about helping you accomplish the why. I would encourage you to do this within every area of your ministry. Maybe take a look at services, events, leadership teams, etc., and start thinking about the structures you need to develop now to accomplish all that God will call you to in the future.

Changing the structure

OK, I feel this is a big topic right now in our churches. Let me be very clear here. I believe that sometimes we need to take a good hard look at our systems and structures. And for sure there is truth in the statement *What got us here may not get us there.* However, changing something just to change it or because it's the sexy thing to do is not only immature but can be downright destructive. God has entrusted us to pastor students. That means we have a responsibility to properly steward the student lives we've been entrusted with.

A lot of shifting is happening right now in church culture. My heart is not to criticize anyone else for what they are doing or not doing. However, I do want to challenge you to think a little bigger. One shift is the idea that student ministries aren't relevant to the church any longer. The main justification for this premise is that we now have a lot of cool churches with young pastors and they are more relevant. OK, so let me poke some holes in this notion. In the first place it doesn't matter how young, hip, trendy, or relevant the lead pastor is. My lead pastor is practical and hilarious, but the truth is that I don't know of a church anywhere in the country where the lead pastor is gearing his messages to teens. So even if the lead pastor is funny, young, and trendy, we are still doing our students an injustice because we aren't focusing on the issues that students are dealing with right now. I have heard the argument that students seem older than they did in the past. Let me help you here. They may seem older, but they are less mature. We live in a tech-driven world, and students are being exposed to more and more at younger ages than ever before. This creates the illusion that students are maturing faster. But recent scientific studies show that while adolescence is starting at a younger age, it's also lasting longer than ever before.

When we create fewer environments for students, I think we are missing it, and we are creating long-term effects that the next generation of church leaders will have to deal with. We could take the easy way out and do what is easiest for us or what brings at least a measure of success now. But I don't believe that's on any of our hearts. I think sometimes we try new things without thinking them all the way through. I

It isn't a revelation for most of us that adolescence is the most malleable time in someone's life. I highly recommend the book *Age of Opportunity: Lessons from the New Science of Adolescence* by Dr. Laurence Steinberg. In this book he discusses what scientists refer to as the reminiscence bump. Take a moment and think back over your life. I, like the vast majority of adults, have some memories of early childhood, although these are mostly vague or surrounding significant emotional events. If you skip ahead to the past several years of your life, the same holds true. In fact, if you are like me, you don't remember what happened last week! But when you think about your life between the ages of roughly ten to twenty-five, most of us not only remember more about that phase of our life, but remember it in more vivid detail, even ordinary events. This is because our brains have more plasticity in that season of our life. When I first heard of this I thought, "Well, wait…Plastic is hard!" But the word *plasticity* here refers to something that's like plastic before it's molded into its final form. In essence, our minds are the most moldable when we're teens, and the older we get, the harder or less moldable our minds become. If that is true, and a lot of significant and compelling research says it is, why would we stop offering environments where students are having positive experiences that are not only relevant to the season where they find themselves now, but also helping to shape them into who they will become?

What I am about to say will no doubt step on some toes, but maybe it's because some of us are too concerned with instant results or feeling pressure from our leadership to produce numbers. Some are more worried about being able to post on social media about how many students showed up to an event we hosted than they are about the real long-term effects our events have on our students. If our student ministry structure is built around what we want, what makes us happy, what strokes our ego, rather than what's best for our students, we are missing the mark.

Listen, you need to develop a structure that works within the context of your culture and your lead pastor's vision for the church. I simply want to encourage you to always filter every major structural decision through the lens of what's best for your students. I feel the need to remind you all that sometimes what's best for them isn't always what they want or ask for! In the church world, the customer *isn't* always right! If they were, we would constantly be changing what we were doing: "The music's too loud," "We need pews," "The preacher's too young," etc. Leadership means that we see further than others, and we have to be willing to sometimes make unpopular decisions for the greater long-term good!

I am a systems and structures guy! I love the old saying that people don't plan to fail, they fail to plan. This is definitely true in the youth ministry world. There have been seasons in which I have elevated the systems and structures over the people. I think the best way to avoid this scenario is to always remember that that the systems and structures exist to help us better take care of people. If you always remember the WHY behind them, you will be less likely to elevate them over the people.

I will conclude this chapter with this last thought: Be intentional with building your student ministry systems and structures. Don't just copy something that works in another culture and try to make it fit in yours. At the same time, don't reinvent the wheel just to reinvent it. The tendency sometimes is to keep coming up with a new structure every couple of years to keep things fresh and new. The problem with that mentality is that we are creating unnecessary chaos in our student ministries. (If you've forgotten why this is a bad thing, please reread chapter 1.) There may come a time when you need to change a structure. But honestly, I believe that's always the last thing you should change. If you are not experiencing growth in an area or in the student ministry as a whole, first you need to ask yourself, "Am I doing everything I should to be doing?" If the answer is yes and the ministry is still struggling, a harder question follows: "Am I in the right seat on the bus?" If the answer is yes, then it's time to look at the structure of your student ministry. Bottom line: be very intentional before you start making structural changes.

Structures are important because they will help you to pastor and lead better. Again, remember that the structure isn't the win, it exists to help you win! If you're not a systems and structures kind of person, make sure to find team members who can help you think this way.

10

Intentional longevity

You know, when I was just getting my feet wet in ministry, one of my mentors told me that I should treat it like a marathon and not a sprint. Truth is, I have never run in a marathon or anything even close. I really need a good reason to run, such as…if I am being chased by a swarm of bees, I will run. Or if I am being chased by a pack of wild dogs or a bear. Pretty much anything that can inflict serious harm to my body would be motivation to run. Or I guess if my wife or kids were in danger I would think about running! Even though I am not much of a runner, I do understand that the way you condition yourself for a marathon is quite a bit different from how you condition yourself for a sprint. I've seen too many people who go into ministry with passion but fizzle out and don't last because they have failed to see student ministry as a marathon. I believe that as pastors and leaders, if we are going to stay where God has called us, we need to not only understand that it's a marathon, but learn how to condition ourselves for the marathon. The Apostle Paul reminds us of this;

"Do you not know that in a race all the runners run, but only one gets the prize? Run in such a way as to get the prize. Everyone who competes in the games goes into strict training. They do it to get a crown that will not last, but we do it to get a crown that will last forever. Therefore I do not run like someone running aimlessly; I do not fight like a boxer beating the air. No, I strike a blow to my body and make it my slave so that after I have preached to others, I myself will not be disqualified for the prize."
1 Corinthians 9:24–27 (NIV)

When we make the choice to pursue God's purpose for our life, we will face opposition. There are going to be times in life when you'll want to quit. When you'll want to give up or just throw in the towel. If I am being honest with you, there have been moments when I have questioned it all. When people questioned my decisions and motives. When people I'd poured a lot into fell away. When I had to do things I didn't want to or didn't sign up for. When I felt burned out from giving so much. When I felt alone and distant from God. When I felt as if what I did went unnoticed. When I realized I would be working every weekend for the rest of my life!

We've all seen and even been close to those who have quit ministry because of moral failure, burnout, being hurt by leadership, working crazy hours for no pay, giving so much of their life to ministry that their marriages and families fell apart. Research group Barna has discovered some really alarming statistics:

> In America nearly four thousand churches close their doors each year.
> 40 percent of pastors quit, most of them in their first five years.
> 33 percent who walk away from ministry don't use their gifts in the local church any longer.
> 7 percent don't even attend church any longer.

Barna also says that the average stay of a youth pastor right now is about ten months. This statistic is unfortunate, and while I don't claim to know all the circumstances driving this stat, I do know that you can't build anything in ten months.

Ministry is rewarding, and being a leader within the body of Christ is very fulfilling if that's what you're called to do. If you're reading this, you probably wouldn't change that for anything in this world! I sometimes feel like Peter, who said to Jesus, "Where else would we go?"

When faced with challenges, most people quit. And far too often they quit one day too soon. I remember that during the first few years of my church I really struggled because I was working crazy hours with very little pay. I had many conversations in those early years with friends and family who encouraged me to leave and find a job at another church. I never did, because I knew that even though things were difficult, this was where God had called me to be. Looking back now I see that I would have missed out on everything God has done here if I had walked away.

Listen, you will never build a healthy and successful student ministry if you are jumping to another church every year or two.

> **Part of being a leader is dealing with discouragement. How you deal with it will determine your longevity and success in ministry**

One of my favorite scriptures is Galatians 6:9–10 (MSG): *"So let's not allow ourselves to get fatigued doing good. At the right time we will harvest a good crop if we don't give up, or quit. Right now, therefore, every time we get the chance, let us work for the benefit of all, starting with the people closest to us in the community of faith."*

If you decide to follow Christ and the purpose He has for your life, you will face hardships. It's really not a question of if but of when. There are going to be times in life and in student ministry when you'll want to quit. What you do in those moments will be what defines your success or failure as a youth pastor.

People start a new year determined to quit smoking, diet, go to the gym, etc....and most of them quit before they ever see results. If I had quit youth ministry after the first parent complained, I would have lasted less than a month. If I had decided to throw in the towel after the first student made me feel like an idiot, I would have lasted a week. If I had walked away the first time I made a mistake, I would have lasted about one day. If I had abandoned youth ministry the first time I felt inadequate, I would have quit before I ever started. One of my favorite definitions of courage is "the quality of mind enabling one to face danger or hardship resolutely." *(Webster's College Dictionary 2010)* It takes courage to stay where God has called you, but the payoff in the end is well worth it. You can't always control your circumstances, but you can control your responses to them.

Eighty percent of seminary and Bible school graduates who enter the ministry will leave within the first five years. Please don't be one of those statistics! Too many students need what you have to offer.

So how do we condition ourselves for the marathon?

Balance

This is one of the main reasons people quit youth ministry. If you are going to stay in it for the long haul, you've got to have balance in your life. If you had asked me at any point over the last sixteen-plus years of doing youth ministry what the most important thing in my life was, I would have said God. But truth is, that hasn't always been the case. There have been times when God has taken a back seat to ministry. There have been times when I have been on the stage preaching to students about the importance of having a healthy relationship with God and feeling like a complete hypocrite because my own relationship with God wasn't what it should be. If God is first in our life, that needs to be evident in our personal relationship with Him. Too often I have done ministry from the reserve of what God has done in my life in the past instead of allowing ministry to come from the overflow of what God is currently doing in my life. Balance is key, and if we don't maintain a healthy relationship with God, how effective will we be at raising up students to live in a healthy and thriving relationship with God? I know some would argue that there is no balance in life or ministry. Some would even say that Jesus wasn't balanced. I disagree! While Jesus was always about putting people first, He also made it a point to get away from people and make sure he was connecting with God. Consider the following passages:

- ◊ John 4: Jesus spends forty days alone in the wilderness.
- ◊ Luke 5: Tells us that Jesus <u>often</u> withdrew to lonely places to pray.
- ◊ Mark 1: Jesus goes off to a solitary place to pray.
- ◊ Mark 3: Jesus withdraws from his disciples.
- ◊ Matthew 14: Jesus goes to a mountainside to pray alone and stays all night.

There were times when He was seeking solitude and the crowds followed and he put the people first. But let's be clear: Jesus modeled this idea of balance and of making sure that he was leading from a place of health.

Maybe for you it's not the personal relationship with God that has suffered, but the relationship with your family. The Bible tells us that we have no business leading others if our own family isn't in order. Yet oftentimes our marriages and families end up being casualties of the ministry. We've got to have balance in our family life. When we make the choice to make ministry a priority over our families, we are not only missing the mark, we are jeopardizing our family for the sake of the ministry. How effective will you really be as a pastor and leader if your marriage is falling apart and your kids hate God and the church because they are to blame for your absence in their lives? It's easy to let every one of our nights fill up doing ministry, and it's not that our ministry isn't important, but our families have to come first. This is something that I think about often. I would hate to wake up one day knowing there are people who love me because I am there for them, but that my family despises me because I am never there for them.

One of my greatest failures in the area of balance has been with my own physical health. Early on in ministry I allowed myself to get so busy that I neglected my own health. Maybe you are thinking that's not that big a deal. I have actually heard leaders say things like, "I will work out when I get to heaven." To me that's foolish! Because truth is, if we are not being good stewards of our own bodies, how long will we be able to effectively reach the students God has called us to lead? I got to the point where I was substantially overweight, had high blood pressure, was stressed all the time, and got sick frequently, and that was at the old age of twenty-five! Sad, right? In order for us to have longevity in our ministry and leadership, we have to make our physical health a priority. If we are not taking care of our bodies by eating right, exercising, and resting, what message are we communicating to those we are leading?

Again, I am not saying I have been perfect at staying balanced; honestly, I was really bad at it early on in ministry. And even now I find that it's more of a process than a destination. I am frequently adjusting and evaluating areas of my life so I can keep some kind of balance. Which is why I want to stress how important this is. If you want to have longevity and sustainable success in youth ministry, please figure out how to have some balance in your life.

Focus

You're the youth pastor, but you're also the janitor, sound guy, kids' director, worship leader, outreach planner…Sound familiar? I know that when we launched the church I had to wear multiple hats. In fact I have been all of the above plus drummer, music coordinator, sign and promotions guy, and facilities setup person, just to name a few. And while there are seasons when you might have to wear multiple hats, you have to be willing to say NO! Someone is always going to want you to do something for them, and we should absolutely be willing to help out across ministries—just don't do it at the cost of your ministry area or your own personal health and balance. I have had to learn how to say no to some good things so that I can say yes to better things. Staying focused on what you're called to do is vital in order to have longevity in ministry. Don't be a jack-of-all-trades and a master of none! Anytime I say yes to something I am saying no to another. Effective leaders have to make sure they are saying yes to the right things. Otherwise you will spend your entire life being OK at a lot of things and never really mastering anything. I don't know about you, but I know what God has called me to do, and at the end of the day I'd rather be excellent at that one thing than be mediocre at a lot of other things that He hasn't called me to do.

Guard Your Heart

Above all else, guard your heart,
For everything you do flows from it.
Proverbs 4:23 (NIV)

I can't overstate the importance of this section! Life in general will give you opportunities to be offended, and ministry will give you even more. If you want to have any kind of longevity in ministry, you have to make sure you are guarding your heart from offense. Over the years I have had multiple opportunities in ministry to get offended, and I have sadly seen too many pastors and leaders, some of whom I was close to, burn out, quit, or disqualify themselves because they held on to offense.

There will be times when people question your actions, your results, and, worse, your motives and integrity. People will say things about you that aren't true or that have only a shred of truth in them. People will undermine your leadership, and probably there will be times when people question the legitimacy of your calling. In those moments you will be faced with a choice. This choice will determine your longevity in ministry. If you allow yourself to be easily offended, you will miss out on everything that God wants to do in and through you. Please, please, please DON'T BE EASILY OFFENDED! There is too much for you to accomplish. There is too much that God wants to do in and through you. Guard your heart above all else. Don't let offense in. When you face those moments in ministry I want to encourage you to check your heart. Take it to God. And then keep going.

The other side of guarding our hearts is about personal integrity. One of the most disheartening things I have experienced in ministry is seeing peers and friends fall into sin and disqualify themselves from ministry. It breaks my heart because the "callings of God are irrevocable," which means that even if you do something to disqualify yourself, you still have a calling that you now can't live out. If you are young in ministry I want to encourage you to deal with character issues now. It's a much bigger deal for a skyscraper to fall than a one-story building. I want to encourage you never to forget where you came from. I think moral failure often starts with pride. And when pride takes root, it opens the door for moral failure. Don't be a celebrity and not a pastor. The most dangerous time in your ministry is when you are experiencing success, because it's easy to get to a place where you start to justify sin in your life. You might start to think, "I am doing so many great things for God, what's the big deal? It's just a little sin." if you ever get to a place where you start thinking like that, get your heart right. That is a dangerous place to be, and we can't afford any more casualties in ministry.

And then make sure that you…

Stay at Jesus's Feet
I can't stress this enough. It's easy to allow other things to come between you and your relationship with God. I know because over the years I have. But if we are going

to have longevity in student ministry, we need to make sure that we are staying at Jesus's feet.

In a recent survey Barna discovered that only 26 percent of pastors said they regularly had personal devotions and felt they were adequately fed spiritually. Nearly 72 percent stated that they studied the Bible only when they were preparing for sermons or lessons. Ouch, that hurts, because I have been that guy. Me preparing a message or teaching for my students or leaders isn't me spending quality time with God. I don't know how you operate, but I am a very practical kind of guy and I like things done the right way. Which is good, but sometimes I jump in and start making decisions for my life and ministry without really seeking God on it. Sometimes in the name of order and excellence in a service or event I have not left any room for God to do his thing. If we are going to effectively lead the students God has called us to lead, we have to make sure we are leading students from the position at Jesus's feet. In John 15:5 we are reminded by Jesus, "Yes, I am the vine; you are the branches. Those who remain in me, and I in them, will produce much fruit. For apart from me you can do nothing."

How often do we try to be the producers of fruit? We are not called to be the ones who produce the fruit. We are called to stay connected with Christ, to follow him and do what He's doing. Then He will bring the fruit in our lives and ministries.

My prayer for you is that no matter where you find yourself in the youth ministry journey—whether you're just starting out, a seasoned veteran, or somewhere in the middle—you will be intentional with the young people God has entrusted you with. This is so much bigger than just our own ministries or personal legacies. The most unreached groups in the world are those under the age of thirty, and in the United States we are literally one generation away from becoming a postmodern Europe. Let's make a choice to lead and build our ministries with intentionality.

Matt Moore

If you're looking for additional resources, coaching, or consulting to help your ministry become more intentional. Or if you are interested in being a part of a youth pastor round table in your area, visit

www.intentionalyouth.com

Printed by Amazon Italia Logistica S.r.l.
Torrazza Piemonte (TO), Italy